WASHINGTON

wild and beautiful

photography by CHARLES GURCHE

FARCOUNTRY
PRESS

Right: Sunrise over Reflection Lake in Mount Ranier National Park.

Front cover: Lupine in Mount Rainier National Park.

Back cover: Dawn at Point of Arches, Olympic National Park.

Title page: Skagit River Valley tulip fields.

ISBN 1-56037-220-6
Photographs © Charles Gurche
© 2002 Farcountry Press

For more information on our books write: Farcountry Press, P.O. Box 5630, Helena, MT 59604; call (800) 821-3874; or visit www.farcountrypress.com

Created, produced, and designed in the United States. Printed in China.

08 07 06 05 04   2 3 4 5

Foreword

Deep in an ancient coastal forest at daybreak, a hermit thrush sang its pure, melodic notes, and they echoed through the trees. A new Washington day was dawning. Surf pounded the shoreline at La Push, sending slow motion blasts of saltwater into the morning sky. A layer of gold mist covered Granite Lake in Eastern Washington, concealing grebes and mergansers. On Mount Rainier's 14,410-foot summit, the first rays of the rising sun turned its glaciers crimson. Ripples on the Columbia River sparkled like camera flashes. Dew glistened in the mountain meadows of the Cascades. From the Palouse to the Pacific, the land was renewed by the morning light.

My first visit to Washington was a summer trip twenty-five years ago. With six friends, our gear, and a dog crammed into a station wagon, we roamed the West for six weeks and 5,000 miles. One lasting memory was a stop at the Hoh Rain Forest in Olympic National Park. We had all grown up near the oak forests and farm country in the Midwest, and this rain forest was completely out of our experience. What began as a walk beneath the towering old growth ended up as an unplanned version of hide and seek, each of us spying and hiding from someone else while silently moving over the mossy ground. At times we separated and took in the power of that magic, mossy forest. Cedars and hemlock 700 years old lured us deeper into the forest.

Throughout Washington there are so many places that hold amazing, unique qualities. Solitude abounds in much of the country of Eastern Washington. When you look closely at the topographic maps, you'll find miles of canyons, cliffs, and potholes out in the basalt rock. At Palouse Falls State Park, the Palouse River rushes through a deep canyon with 100-foot falls. Ridges above the Yakima River bloom with a great variety of desert flowers. The list goes on: Philleo Lake, Riverside Hills State Park, the swales of Garfield County, all fine places to spend a spring afternoon. There are the Cascade Mountains, and the beauties of Wenatchee National Forest, Early Winter Spires in Okanogan National Forest, and rolling Kittatas County.

This collection of images is just a tiny glimpse of the Washington landscape. I've attempted to capture a bit of the magic that I sense while in these outdoor places. At times I wonder about the fate of some of these areas and hope that the images may help to strengthen our desire to honor and preserve such a valuable entity. As stewards of the land, we hold a huge responsibility to ensure the continuance of this great gift.

—Charles Gurche

Above: Patterson Lake in the Methow Valley wears autumn aspen colors.

Facing page: Yellow fawn lily grows at Maple Pass, North Cascades National Park.

Above: An Orcas beach monolith.

Facing page: Juniper Dunes National Wilderness Area's
7,000 acres protect a large variety of birds and mammals.

Left: Eastern Washington's Granite Lake on a stormy day.

Below: Mount Si in King County, whited out with snow.

Above: At Seattle's Maritime Heritage Center, the Center for Wooden Boats exhibits authentic and reproduction craft beginning with Native American and Polynesian canoes.

Facing page: Along the Ohanapecosh River.

Above: Naturally flocked ponderosa pine in Spokane County.

Left: Sunset, Olympic coast.

Above: San Juan Island Historical Museum, Friday Harbor.

Facing page: Hawthorn leaves in frost.

Above: Lopez Island's south shore.

Facing page: Griffith Bay, San Juan Island National Historical Park.

Right: Grasses and common alkanet.

Below: Red paintbrush, yellow balsamroot, and purple lupine blossoms in the Columbia River Gorge.

Facing page: Young wheat in the Palouse Country.

Left: Coleman Glacier on 10,778-foot-tall Mount Baker.

Below: Kittitas County.

Above: Orcas Island starfish.

Right: Tidepool near Copalis Beach.

Fog fills in the gaps of the Tatoosh Range.

Above: Palouse Falls sparkles in Franklin County.

Right: Day's end near Eagle Point in Olympic National Park.

Above: Hummel Lake, Lopez Island.

Right: White River Park in Mountain Rainier National Park.

Mount Rainier's south face,
lit by dawn.

Arrowleaf balsamroot and aspen in the Okanogan National Forest.

Right: Black oak leaves amidst the reeds.

Below: Twisp River reflections.

Above: Frenchman Coulee in eastern Washington's Scablands.

Facing page: Wheat harvest time in the Palouse.

Mount Adams, rising above its namesake wilderness.

Left: A blockhouse and formal garden at English Camp, San Juan Island National Historical Park, were built by British Royal Marines.

Below: Yakima County peach orchard poetry.

Near Hole in the Wall, Olympic National Park.

Seattle skyline from West Seattle.

Above: In the Riverside Hills, eastern Washington.

Right: Mount Baker, a slumbering volcano, occasionally lets off some steam.

Above: Caskey Lake in the Cascade Range.

Facing page: Olympic National Park's Marymere Falls.

Above: Winter twilight in Mount Spokane State Park.

Right: Mount Shuksan in the North Cascades.

Above: Gifford Pinchot National Forest symmetry.

Facing page: Crooked Creek in the Bird Creek Meadows near Mount Adams.

Left: Windy Ridge in Mount St. Helens National Volcanic Monument at sunrise.

Below: Reflections tint Tipsoo Lake, Mount Rainier National Park.

Above: Granite Lake in eastern Washington

Facing page: Mount Pilchuck in its namesake state park at sunset.

Above: Construction of the Garfield County Courthouse, Pomeroy, began in 1901.

Left: The landmark Beacon Rock along the Columbia River.

Above: At Green Bluff.

Facing page: White poplars on Browne Mountain, Spokane County.

Above: Western pasqueflowers and lupine on Naches Peak.

Facing page: Mount Baker Wilderness snowfield.

Above: Moonrise over the Cowlith Chimneys.

Facing page: Manito Boulevard in Spokane.

Right: The mighty Columbia River flowing to the sea.

Below: Dayton's historical train depot was built in the late 1800s by Oregon Rail & Navigation Company, and moved to its present site by the Union Pacific.

The Snake River passes through Garfield County.

Spokane's Comstock Park.

me Kiln Lighthouse
San Juan Island.

Above: The Spokane River, Riverside State Park.

Facing page: Liberty Bell Mountain and the Early Winter Spires
are in Okanogan National Forest.

Above: Vine maples flame in Stevens Canyon, Mount Rainier National Park.

Right: Bluffs along the Columbia.

Fog fills Mount Moran State Park on Orcas Island.

Union Station in Tacoma, under its copper dome, opened in 1911 to serve train passengers.

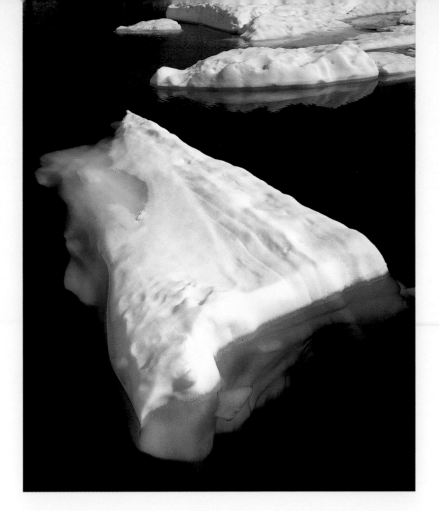

Right: Iceberg floats loose in the Cascades' Bagley Creek.

Below: Pink mountain heather brightens North Cascades National Park.

Facing page: Comet Falls, Mount Rainier National Park.

Above: In Columbia County.

Left: Columbia River Gorge National Scenic Area extends for about eighty miles.

76   Doe Bay off Orcas Island, at dawn.

Left: Skagit
River Valley
tulip nursery.

Facing page:
Thunder Lake
in the North
Cascades.

Right: Rosario Strait, viewed from Orcas Island.

Below: Bullrushes on Philleo Lake, eastern Washington.

Above: Western serviceberry grows along Lake Chelan.

Facing page: In the Washington State Capitol, Olympia.

Above: Strands of kelp washed ashore.

Left: Surf-polished pebbles near La Push.

Facing page: The beach at American Camp, San Juan Islands.

Above: A warm holiday welcome in Spokane.

Facing page: Sunrise from the top of Mount Constitution,
in Mount Moran State Park on Orcas Island.

Left: Historic fire truck at Liberty.

Below: Rosalia's railroad bridge.

Facing page: Klickitat County meadow abloom.

Above: The Grande Ronde River Canyon.

Facing page: Near Ellensburg.

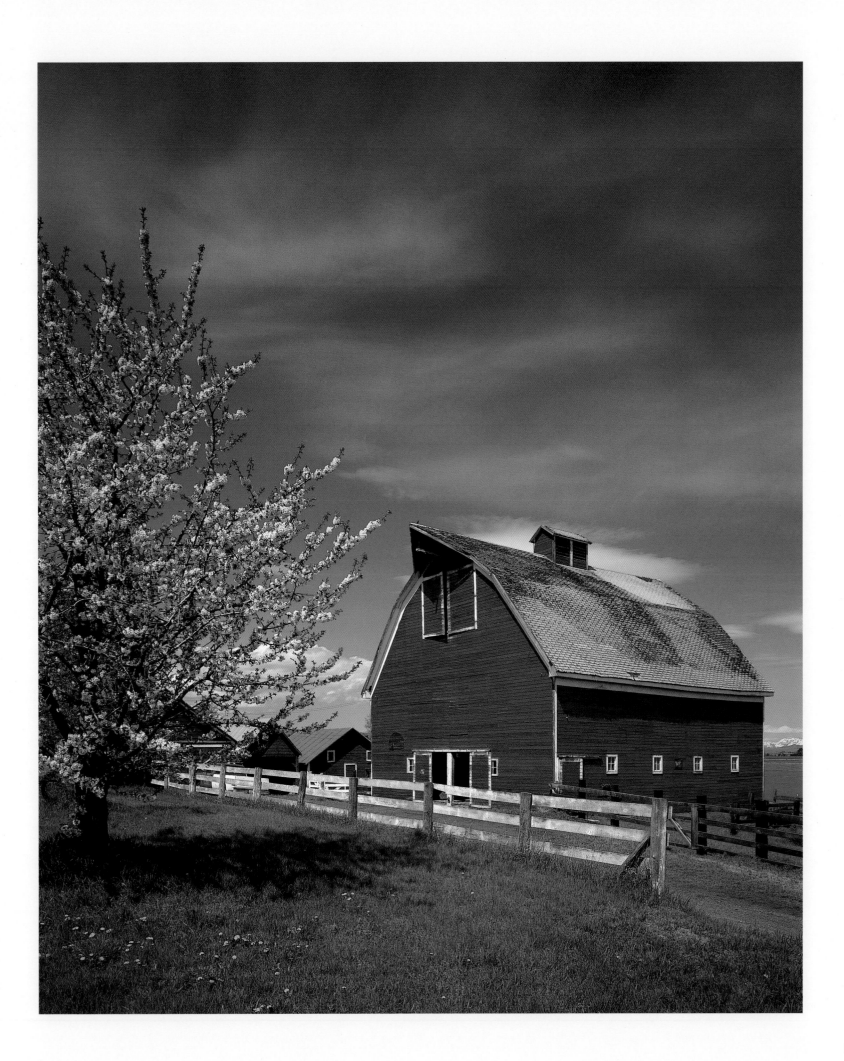

Left: The Wenatchee River near Leavenworth.

Below: Peaceful grove of aspens.

Above: Robin Lake in Alpine Lakes Wilderness Area.

Facing page: Paradise Meadows, Mount Ranier National Park.

Above: Cedar in Mount Rainier National Park's Grove of the Patriarchs.

Facing page: Stony beach at low tide, Orcas Island.

Wenatchee National Forest sandstone formations.

Right: Oregon sunshine grows near the Columbia.

Below: Downtown Ellensburg.

Above: Aubretia flourishes in Spokane County.

Left: A field of penstemon in Mount St. Helens National Volcanic Monument.

Above: A morning fog halo in the Olympic rain forest.

Right: Surf's up near La Push.

The ragged profile of Silver Star
Mountain in the Cascades.

Left: Washington State Capitol detail.

Below: An alder forest.

Facing page: Huckleberry meadow in autumn beneath the Tatoosh Range.

Left: Bigleaf maples in mossy dress, Hoh Rain Forest.

Facing page: Cold meltwater sheeting over a cascade below Mount Rainier.

Above: Lupine rebounds after Wenatchee National Forest's Chelan Fire.

Left: Lavender sunset in the coastal portion of Olympic National Park.

A meadow of western pasque-flowers in the Cascade Mountains.

Above: Aspens raise their leafy spires.

Right: Mount Daniel, Alpine Lakes Wilderness Area.

Above: Summer sky over the rich Palouse.

Facing page: Friday Harbor fishing nets, San Juan Island.

Above: William O. Douglas Wilderness Area honors the memory of a conservationist U.S. Supreme Court justice who often hiked here.

Right: View of sunrise from Sunrise Ridge.

Following page: Point Thomas at Orcas Island.